Whence

A Play

Leo Smith

SAMUEL FRENCH

FOUNDED 1830

SAMUELFRENCH-LONDON.CO.UK
SAMUELFRENCH.COM

ISBN 978-0-573-12300-9

www.samuelfrench-london.co.uk

www.samuelfrench.com

FOR AMATEUR PRODUCTION ENQUIRIES

UNITED KINGDOM AND WORLD
EXCLUDING NORTH AMERICA
plays@SamuelFrench-London.co.uk
020 7255 4302/01

Each title is subject to availability from Samuel French,

depending upon country of performance.

WHENCE

First presented at the Millfield Theatre, Edmonton, London, in March, 1989, with the following cast of characters:

The Woman	Linda Chandler
The Man	Jeff Hammond

Directed by Leo Smith

The play takes place in subterranean chambers

Time——the distant future

Dedicated to my son, Max —
the first play for the firstborn

whence *adv., conj., pron. and noun (arch. or literary.)* **1.** *interrog. adv.* From what place or source? From where? (No one knows whence she came.)

Whence was overall winner in the 25th Southgate Drama Festival and also won the Best Director, Best Actor, Best Actress, Best Southgate Society and Best New Play awards.

WHENCE

Scene 1

The scene is semi-lit and brightens when a lantern is brought on

After some moments the Woman enters from upstage with a lantern. She is aged late thirties to early forties and is a typical earth mother type. She is mature and responsible but displays a fixated sense of motherly love towards the baby. She is dressed in careworn clothes that have obviously been repaired several times but are clean and well-cared for, She hurries to the crib, which is down left, and begins to comfort the baby

Woman There, baby, there. Mummy had to leave you for a little while. But I'm back now and I'm not going out again, oh, for ages and ages. If only you could understand, I've sometimes got to leave you here. It's safest. It's best. Where I go is . . . different and I wouldn't want to leave you behind, which might happen somewhere different. But if you stay here I can always find you again. Just follow the marks I've made on the walls. Sometimes I forget what they're for on the way back. Sometimes even going, but I know if I just keep going I'll get back to my little baby. Always. No one else knows what the marks mean so no one else will ever find this place or you. Especially you. Oh, don't fret, my little one. Mummy's here too. Oh, dear. I know, let me hum to you. Now, what's that song . . . how does it go? Oh, baby, Mummy's memory is getting so bad she can't remember anything anymore. She gets so cross with herself for not being able to think. Try again, think think think think think. (*Pause. She sighs*) How does it go. (*Pause . She shakes her head*) Oh, well. Perhaps I'll just hum. (*She begins to hum tunelessly, rocking the cradle as she does so*)

During the humming the Man enters and stands looking at the Woman. He is a handsome young man in his early to mid-twenties. Short of stature, he is nonetheless confident, intelligent, knowledge-able and extremely self-centred at times. He displays immature attitudes but equally at other times is older than his years

The Woman turns , mid hum, and starts, covering the cot protectively with her arms

Who's there?

The Man takes a pace into the area. The Woman can now see who it is

Oh, it's you. (*She visibly relaxes*)
Man   And who else did you expect? Father Christmas?
Woman Please don't play games with me. I'm tired from walking to the water and back, worried out of my mind about what if someone should walk in and find the baby and take him away. I'll die if that happened, you know that, I'd just lay down and die.

Pause

Man   No one is going to find the baby. No one is going to find you, this chamber, or me. I've told you on many, many, many occasions there is no one else in this complex of tunnels for several hundred miles. Except us. You and me. Incarcerated in this dark tomb waiting for the water to run out or the food tubes to finally pack up or the internal nuclear fision that lights and heats us to go out like a candle. Then we would surely expire from exposure or hypothermia in a matter of days.

Pause

Woman And the baby.
Man What?
Woman The baby, don't forget the baby.
Man No. No, that's right. (*Distracted, he turns and looks at the cot*)
  We musn't forget the baby.

Some moments

Woman(*smiling and standing*) Did you get far today?
Man No, there's been another cave-in on level seven. I couldn't go
  my usual way. Had to double back, go up to level six just to get to
  section eight ventilation control airlock. Just got to level six and had
  to turn back at once because of gas leaking. I only managed to get
  through the airlock before the automatic system became operational.
  Until the purification drones clear level six we're locked in again.
Woman Did you find anything?
Man No, there were some interesting rubbish chutes that could yield
  one or two useful items. Most things seem to crumble in your hands,
  though, being originally made of strengthened biodegradeable de-
  rivatives, not anything proper, built to last, like plastic.
Woman Why do you like plastic?
Man I don't really. However, when I was a child, there was not a
  natural material left in the world to make things like furniture out of.
  So they turned out furniture made of synthetic materials in large
  quantities. Even made cars totally from plastic once.
Woman What's a car?
Man (*continuing without answering her question*) So when the
  synthetics ran out they melted them all down, mixed them with this
  degradeable derivative and now "poof" it's all breaking down to
  nothing. Start with nothing but a pile and end up with a pile of nothing,
  one scientist said at the time. No one listened, of course, he might not
  know it but he was right and that's a fact.
Woman (*her question forgotten*) I do so like it when you talk of things
  past. Things I've ceased to remember. Things that go back so far I

can't even begin to think how much I know, how little I know and how much I've forgotten. It's almost as if there's a great wedge of nothing on my brain or where my brain should be and nothing I can do or say can bring back the memory of things that once were. All I do know is that you're here and I'm here and baby's here and that's all there is. You know so much. It frightens me sometimes, the things you know and I don't. Where did you learn such things and how come now I know so little? Please say. I'd like you to say. I know you've told me before but I've . . . forgotten. And you talk so nicely and so well. Go on, just for me, tell me again whence and how we came . . .

Pause

Man   Many, many, many years ago there was a world . . . oh, not like this one, the world down here. There was a world above — blue skies, blue seas, sunshine. I wasn't aware of such things myself, having only seen them on videos and photographs. Nevertheless they were there and from what I can gather they were wonderful things to behold. The wind in one's face and the sun on one's back; to walk on the beach — these are experiences I've only witnessed on film, on a screen — a reality I don't know.

Woman   How long have we been here? How long have people been down here?

Man   I don't know exactly. Decades of years.

Woman   But what happened? What went wrong with the blue sea and the blue sky?

Man   I only know what I've been told and what I've seen down here. Up there, according to the videos, the world was filled with millions of people - all races, all creeds. Mostly attempting to live in some form of harmony. Then their leaders. The leaders of these people, these continents, were responsible for their welfare and only their continent alone. This led to problems of communication. What one leader decreed was right and proper for his people hardly ever coincided with the wishes and demands of another continent, thousands of miles away. Oh yes, the balance of economics and ecology became that finely tuned. I can't really explain it *all* again. There's too much to

tell and if I did it would all come out in a rush so your poor muddled
brain would never take it all in.

Woman   And yet I want to. I want to know. I have the right to know.
So I can tell baby when he grows up. Then he can pass it on to his
children.

Man   His children. I sincerely hope there will be world where there will
be more children like him. (*Pause*) Down here now we have light.
Some light. It varies from day to day, hour to hour. There's no
distinction between day and night. Do you know why?

The Woman shakes her head

No, I thought not. It's because somewhere deep within the heart of
this cavernous series of holes we call home, there is a nuclear plant
still going. The light and heat will vary intermittently from time to
time. It's how it is. Sometimes it will be as bright as the sunshine, and
again so very dim you can hardly see your hand in front of your face.

Woman   It's a bit like my memory, my brain. Now well, now failing,
fading. I often can't put one thought in front of another. (*Pause*) It just
goes, the time. I think it's time that I think I remember. The moments
passing. There's baby to look after. I always remember to come back
to baby. Sometimes I think how wonderful it all is, having you and
baby. It's been so long now. I do remember that. But you — you're
so knowledgeable. Why do you know so much?

Man   Well, without going too far back, the reason you are like you are
and I am as I am is genetic engineering. When man was finally forced
underground by reasons I'll come to later, the scientists were in-
structed that the future community should be perfect. There would be
no mistake about who was bred. That's me. I wasn't born, I was
created in a test tube along with thousands of other test-tube babies.
Genetically engineered, brains perfect, physically strengthened to
withstand the pressures of living constantly underground. Subjected
to a certain amount of radiation so that sickness would not come upon
us as quickly as it had our previous generations. You. From the time
I've known you you were, I gather, one of the mothers, genetically
engineered to breed babies. Your body manufactured to be the perfect

surrogate mother for receiving a test tube foetus. To produce healthy babies. Whereas I was bred to be intelligent and logical, you were merely an instrument of the scientists' design. A baby factory.

Pause

The maternal instincts were in-built and enhanced by drugs secretly introduced into your food and drink. All *your* brain was designed to think about was infanticipating and the bringing-up of children until they were ready to be processed on to the next stage of their pre-destined evolution. The drugs I'm referring to were subsequently blamed for many of the mothers suffering from brain damage which rendered their usefulness as caring single unit parents somewhat invalid as they began to lose control of normal bodily functions. *(Pause)* I deeply suspect that this and certain environmental damage has resulted in you suffering from what has become known as the daydrome syndrome. What stage you are at and how far it will develop I can't say. It does, however, explain your growing mental lapses.

Woman You are saying I was deliberately made to feel the way I do?

Man   Of course. This was exactly the effect those who brought us underground wanted to achieve.

Woman But what happened to this world that was genetically engineered? To all the people that were born? To all the mothers. What happened?

Man They died. In droves, in millions. They died.

Woamn But how?

Man   Do you really want to know? *(Pause)* Again, I've told you all this before.

Woman Oh, please let me know. So I can tell baby when he grows up.

Man   So that's your future, is it? How little you know. *(Aside)* I wonder, should I tell you the worst?

Woman What's that? You're talking to yourself again!. More and more lately I've found you talking quietly to yourself.

Man Well, that's not really surprising, is it? I mean there's hardly a roomful of people to circulate around having deep, meaningful conversations. Speaking my thoughts out loud is a sort of therapy. It helps to concentrate my mind on the more important aspects of survival down here. Anyway, you wanted to know why the people died. The truth is, no one really knows. The official explanation was a particularly virulent virus that killed people within hours of contracting it. There was no cure. It was all over in a few weeks. Living down here we were all living too close together.

Woman How did we live though this sickness if it was that bad?

Man Some of us, very few in fact, seemed to get the virus in a very mild form early on. Certainly not bad enough to be a killer. Then, when we did become sick really badly, our bodies had built up enough of their own immunity against the virus, that we didn't die. Though whether this is a blessing or not I now sometimes wonder.

Woman Oh no, don't say that. At least we've some kind of life to look forward to. Especially when it's a good, bright, warm light to bask in.

Man Yes, you're right. It is good to feel alive.

Woman How many people are there left, do you think, down here?

Man Not many. A couple of hundred within a fifteen hundred mile radius of here. Certainly no more than a thousand in the whole of Europe.

Woman You've met some of these people. Talked with them? Seen what they've got in store?

Man They didn't let me get close. Too dangerous, they said. "Sod off - or you'll get a cross-bow bolt between your shoulder blades!" "OK, OK", I said, and retreated quickly.

Woman You've told me of the recent happenings. What I've forgotten is why we had to come down underground in the first place? What drove us into this cave-like existence?

Man (*sighing*) I really don't think you'd understand.

Woman Try me. Perhaps I'm in one of my more lucid brain periods.

Man All right. Though you'll probably have forgotten again in half an hour's time.

Woman Probably. But that's half the fun, now. Just hearing you retell the stories passes the time so well.

Man CFCs.

Woman What?

Man That's the reason — CFCs — man had to live underground. He had no choice in the end, except stay on the top and fry.

Woman I don't understand. And don't tell me that I wouldn't. Please try and explain a little clearer.

Man (*laughing*) All right. Well, as I've already talked about, the earth had an atmosphere long ago. A beautiful, clean, blue, heaithy wind and cloud laden atmosphere. Then mid-way through the 20th century a group of scientists noticed that the atmosphere around the South polar region had worn thin, causing a window effect that was allowing cancer-causing ultra-violet rays on to the earth's atmosphere. Research showed that this window effect had been caused by the release of ozone-depleting chlorofluro carbon gases. CFCs to you. These were present in items widely used at the time and were increasingly polluting the atmosphere. Some governments heeded the dire warnings of the environmental scientists and banned their use altogether. However, other countries, including China, chose to ignore all pleas for a safer, healthier earth and produced so much that the "window" on the South Pole just grew and grew. It was only a question of years before the atmosphere was totally polluted The surface of the earth was becoming no longer tenable by man and therefore had to move into this mole-like existence underground. Huge bunkers were built to house the population and then came the genetic engineering. Those countries whose leaders were not wise or simply could not afford to move the whole population underground simply perished without trace. That's why we are never cold in here and it is always illuminated to a greater or lesser degree. They left vast areas of solar panelling on the surface that provides us with all the heat we could ever need. Now there's hardly anyone to use it and the earth had to die to provide it. (*Pause*) There, that's the lesson for tonight. Time for rest and sleep for all of us.

Woman Do you remember that song you taught me months ago? You said it was a lull or something? Anyway, it was for me to sing baby to sleep.

Man Yes, of course I remember. I'll go through the words again and then the tune for you to pick up.

> So good-night, now, once more,
> With roses roof'd over
> All tied up with bows
> Slip under the clothes.
>
> When the morning shall break,
> Full of joy you will wake,
> When the morning shall break,
> Full of joy you shall wake.

The Woman begins singing slowly with assistance from the Man

She rocks the cradle

The Man picks up the lantern. He turns to go then looks back at the Woman who is singing

The Man exits

The Woman finishes singing

Black-out

SCENE 2

The next day

Bright sunny atmosphere in total contrast to the preceeding ending. The Lights fade throughout the scene

The Woman runs on, visibly happy and contented, laughing and chuckling. The baby is forgotten. She is followed by the Man who is in the same mood

The Man goes to catch her. She evades him. They play like children. Eventually he catches her and she manoeuvres around so she is embracing him

Woman *(holding him)* Oh, what a good day. The light so bright, the air so clean. It almost feels like there's one of those breezes that you described to me. *(She sighs contentedly)* Days like this should go on for ever and ever. Me and my boys together.

Man *(breaking away and pretending to pick flowers)* Look, here are some primroses and things.

Woman How beautiful they are. Each individual petal a work of art. Look, such a wondrous sight to behold.

They both look at the bunch of flowers . The Man holds the Woman's hand and puts an arm around her and smiles lustily into her eyes. She smiles sweetly back, not catching the meaning of his intention. He continues to hold her harder

Don't look at me like that!

Man Like what?

Woman You've got something on your mind. I can see it in your eyes. My God, I remember now! *(She tries to break away)*

The Man forces a kiss on her lips. She then, being the physically stronger of the two, throws him off and breaks away

Never do that again, boy.

Man Boy, is it now. What game were you playing just now. Teasing me and leading me on. Not treating me like a boy then, were you ?

Woman I was just being happy. And you've spoilt it. Ruined my beautiful day with your sex.

Man Look, I was just doing what comes naturally. The way you're reacting it's as if a kiss was totally alien to you.

Woman It is. Perhaps you don't know the whole truth about us "mothers", especially as you're such a young boy.

Man Stop calling me a boy! It annoys me intensely. I'll have you know my tutors at University thought my sexual technique the best they'd seen in the procreation classes. A real man in the making, they said.

Woman Just because you were taught sex it doesn't make you a man. Even having it doesn't make you a man.

Man You make sex sound like a dirty word. What is the matter with you?

Woman Can't you guess? You, with your fancy thought processes, obviously can't know everything.

Pause

Well, let me tell you. Let me put you straight on this, boy.

Man Don't . . .

Woman I'll call you what I like. Don't you realize I'm old enough to be your mother. Though God forbid a son of mine should ever turn out like you, assaulting a woman like that. We — mothers, as you rightly call us — never had the academic training in technique. To tell you the truth ,we never had sex. Ever. We were shown educational films of procreation but we all fell about laughing when we saw the antics they were getting up to. You see, no pleasure was allowed us on our begetting. Implantation was often quite painful though this was soon forgotten once conception was confirmed. I don't have any emotional or physical experience of advances and "kissing". To me, I felt dead when you did that thing to me, I feel dirty and soiled because that side of life was forbidden the mothers. I've had seven children and never had intercourse in my life. And you ask me what's wrong? The way I've been conditioned, that's what's wrong, boy.

The Man goes for her, slaps her round the face, forces her down. He straddles her

Man I'll show you who you're calling a boy. (*He hits her again*) You won't be doing it again in a hurry.

The Woman screams and struggles

Woman STOP IT! Don't. Don't, PLEASE DON'T. You must stop now. I can't. I'm not able to. I've been operated on. I'm not physically capable. *(She throws him off)*

The Man squirms on the side of the stage

They removed all my sexual organs. You're wasting your time. Leave me, please leave me alone.

Man *(subdued)* I'm sorry. I didn't know. I just didn't know. Oh, God, what have I done?

The Woman recovers herself

Woman They told us about men in the ward. Men who preyed on women, men who abused women, beat them and raped them. I never heard, though, of women abusing men, women abusing other women. *(To herself)* Is it really only men who do such unbearable things?

There is a long pause

(Going to the crib and rocking the baby) There, there, Mummy's all right now. I had a tiff with a man but it's all right now.

Pause

Man I'm not like that. I'm not one of those men you describe. I don't know why that happened. Mental abberation you'd call it, I suppose. Don't you know that I'm really the sort of loving person you've come to know over the past few months.

Woman Love? What do you know of love?

Man Only what I was taught. . .

Woman *(overlapping)* Only what I was taught . . . Is that your only experience of love? Listen, when I was on my fifth child, I was given the choice of leaving the mothers. I didn't. I'll tell you why. I loved my children. When you see your tiny baby strengthen and grow big and strong over the years, it affects you in a way you can't really put into so many words. To nurture them when poorly and teach them rudimentary first steps in life, you don't know what that means to a mother. But where, you ask, does love come into this? To me it was the realization of choice. I wanted to go on in spite of the fact that at the age of five the children were then taken away. I knew in my heart of hearts that I would always love them and they me. When they went, another egg was found for me. Another baby. More caring, more love. When you carry on loving even though the object is taken away, that to me is love. And if you're lucky enough to ever feel that way about someone and have that love returned to you then you'll know . . .

Pause

Man Don't you see? You were created to think that.
Woman No, and I never will.
Man (*sighing*) It's all pretend.
Woman You say it's pretend, but it's all we've got. At least I've got baby.
Man Baby. The baby is the biggest sham of all (*He moves towards the crib*)
Woman Don't you touch him!
Man There's nothing to touch. He doesn't EXIST. (*He grabs the bundle from the cot and struggles with the Woman*)

The bundle falls apart and the Man flings the clothes away

There, end of pretence, no more kidding yourself, baby is gone. Caput. Finito.
Woman (*sobbing*) No! He's not! He's real, he's mine!
Man Stop it, stop the dream and we can start living real lives with no pretence and no baby.
Woman (*wrapping "baby" back into shape*) There, there, hush, hush. You'll be better soon, no more pain. Let Mummy kiss it better.
Man (*aside*) Oh, Jesus, this will never end.

He holds out his hands to the Woman

Woman Don't come near me.

The Man moves in

I said, don't even think about it.
Man But we've only got one another.
Woman You don't even have that now.

The Woman leaves

The Man holds his head, kneels down and sobs

After some moments there is a Black-out

The Man exits in the Black-out

SCENE 3

Several weeks later

The scene opens on a bare stage with the light at a "dull" level

The Woman comes on with the baby and puts him into the crib with cooing sounds

The Man appears and stands looking. He is holding something. After some moments the Woman looks up gives him a half smile and returns her attention to the crib

Man I've brought you a present. Actually it's for both of you. I've been working at it for ages, looking for bits of metal and rag in the waste chutes. Then yesterday I found the musical bit. It was quite by chance really, under some old rotting infant clothes. I wondered if it all came from a nursery. (*He holds out the mobile and shows how it should go round*)

Woman What is it? I've never seen such a thing.

Man It's called a mobile. They were attached to the sides of cots to help tiny babies to go to sleep and give then a point of visual interest. This one's broken, though, so I don't quite know how we're going to attach it to the crib.

Woman I'm sure we'll find a way, won't we, baby? Yes, we will, we will.

The Man brings the mobile over and attempts to attach it to the side of the crib but doesn't seem to be able to do so

Here, let me try. (*She does so and after a few moments the mobile is suspended from the side of the crib*) Oh, it's beautiful! It's the best thing you've made since you put the crib together.

The Man goes to the mobile

Man Here, let me show you how it works (*He winds the mobile up - not too much*)

The Woman is clearly excited by the movement and sound

Woman What a lovely, lovely thing. You're such a clever boy to make this for Mummy and baby.

Man Don't you remember the tune?

Woman No, I can't recall. You know I can't remember anything from one minute to the next. If my head wasn't on my shoulders I'd leave it somewhere.

Man It's the one I taught you some weeks ago. Can't you try and remember the words? I'll help you start off.

The Man starts to sing some words. The Woman joins in falteringly at first, then remembering more and more

Woman Yes, yes. How did I remember that?

Man An association of words and music. The mind can assimilate such things into the subconcious more easily. Did you know that mixed in to the muzak they played everywhere down here were hidden messages? It's how they stopped individuals from being aggressive and going about killing one another.

If the mobile has stopped then the Woman touches it lovingly. If not, wait for the music to stop

Woman *(getting up)* Do you know what today is?

The Man shakes his head

It's your birthday. Oh, I don't mean your real birthday but the anniversary of your coming here. To us. Look on the wall. I've marked off each light period and now it's exactly one year. I should have made you something instead of you giving me presents.

Man How clever of you to keep count and to keep remembering to mark the wall. Perhaps you're not as ill as I thought.

Woman Ill. I'm not ill. I don't feel any different than I did a year ago.

Man Perhaps not. *(Pause)* There are some things I should tell you now. Perhaps today will be a good day to tell you.

Woman What "things"?

Man The future,

Woman Oh, that. Don't let's talk about that now. I want things just to go on as they are, with you, me and baby. Going on from light to light. We've managed for a year to eke out our existence together. Why can't we just go on and on doing the same?

Man You have got to face up to reality and the time is now.

Woman But . . .

Man Please don't interrupt. Let me speak for a few moments.

Woman All right. But no more talk of killings and things. It quite upsets me.

Pause

Man I cannot discuss the future without speaking of death. But not the end. Think of this as a new begining.

Woman Death. Whose? Certainly not mine or yours. We'll go on and on. *(She looks at the Man)* Won't we?

The Man shakes his head

Oh, God!

Man You must have suspected yourself for some time but chose to ignore it. You're slowing down and starting to daydream more. The daydream syndrome is affecting you more and more. There's more. The radiation levels are increasing now throughout the lower levels. Your body's immunity is not enough to cope with any increased demands. The sickness will now grow rapidly until you can no longer function normally. It's merely a question of time.

Woman I don't want to die *(Pause)* Not here, not like this. Surely there must be something we can do? Move to a lower level. They go down to level 150, you once said. Come on, let's gather our few belongings together and go now. It won't take long.

Man It would take us days to get down to a safer place. I'm worried you wouldn't last the journey. Besides, taking your child along would slow us down. It would take twice the time. It wouldn't do any good.

Pause

Woman How long have I got?

Man Another couple of months. That is, providing you rest and don't overtax your system and take great care about not drinking contaminated water. The final illness is quite short. Two days at the most. Don't worry, I'll take care of you. You will be as comfortable as I can make you.

Woman I hope it's a bright day with that faint breeze you told me of on the beach. I hope it's a beautiful day. *(Pause)* Who will care for my baby?

Man I will. I'll love him and protect him better than any mother could. Nurture, you said. He'll be the best nurtured baby in the whole wide world. I promise.

They embrace

Woman Hold me. Oh, God, hold me till I break. I've never known anyone quite like you before. We weren't allowed to. You are a beautiful boy. I've often wondered if you could have been a son of mine. (*She sobs*)

Man Stop this now, you'll wake baby and we wouldn't want that.

Woman No, no, you're right. (*She recovers slightly*) What will you do?

Man Try to make contact with another group. Some people who will accept me and baby for what we are. (*Pause*) Perhaps there'll be another mother to love us just the same. But not yet, after all we still have a little time together.

Woman The light's going. End of another light, end of another day. (*She goes to mark the wall*) You will look after him, won't you?

Man Of course. As if he were my own.

Woman He's going to grow up into a big strong boy. He's the future, you know. The future depends on him.

Man Don't worry. The future will be safe with us.

Woman Time to lie down. I'm tired, suddenly very weary. Old and tired and weary. Play the mobile once more before we sleep.

The Man goes and winds up the mobile as they both prepare for sleep

Man Good-night.

Woman Good-night. Hush baby, hush. Sleep well for tonight.

The Woman lies down near the Man

While the mobile is playing the Lights fade to a Black-out. As the mobile finishes we hear a baby start to cry in the darkness

Curtain

FURNITURE AND PROPERTY LIST

On stage: Crib. *In it*: swaddling

Off stage: Lantern (**Woman**)
Mobile (**Man**)

LIGHTING PLOT

One interior. Subterranean chambers

SCENE 1

To open: Semi-darkness

Cue 1 **The Woman** brings a lantern on   (Page 1)
Increase lighting slightly

Cue 2 **The Woman** finishes singing   (Page 9)
Black-out

SCENE 2

To open: Bright, sunny atmosphere. Fading throught scene

*Cue*3 **The Man** kneels and sobs. Some moments   (Page 14)
Black-out

SCENE 3

To open: Dull lighting

Cue 4 **The Woman** lies down   (Page 18)
Black-out

EFFECTS PLOT

Cue 1   As the mobile finishes playing   (Page 18)
          Baby cries

9 780573 123009